T0011462

Making Money

by Jennifer Boothroyd

Consultant: Kari Servais
Middle School Family & Consumer Science Educator

BEARPORT
PUBLISHING

Minneapolis, Minnesota

Credits

Cover and title page, © turk_stock_photographer/iStock; 5, © tap10/iStock; 7, © Wirestock Creators/Shutterstock; 9, © Andrey_Popov/Shutterstock; 11T, © seyomedo/Shutterstock; 11B, © michaeljung/Shutterstock; 13, © gorodenkoff/iStock; 15, © lunopark/Shutterstock; 16–17, © Dragon Images/Shutterstock; 19T, © PV productions/Shutterstock; 19B, © Hryshchyshen Serhii/Shutterstock; 21, © Rawpixel.com/Shutterstock; 23, © Africa Studio/Shutterstock; 24, © Monkey Business Images/Shutterstock; 25, © dc_slim/Shutterstock; and 27, © MillaF/Shutterstock.

Bearport Publishing Company Product Development Team

President: Jen Jenson; Director of Product Development: Spencer Brinker; Senior Editor: Allison Juda; Editor: Charly Haley; Associate Editor: Naomi Reich; Senior Designer: Colin O'Dea; Associate Designer: Elena Klinkner; Associate Designer: Kayla Eggert; Product Development Assistant: Anita Stasson

Library of Congress Cataloging-in-Publication Data

Names: Boothroyd, Jennifer, 1972– author.
Title: Making money / by Jennifer Boothroyd.
Description: Minneapolis, Minnesota : Bearport Publishing Company, [2023] | Series: Personal finance: need to know | Includes bibliographical references and index.
Identifiers: LCCN 2022029717 (print) | LCCN 2022029718 (ebook) | ISBN 9798885094177 (library binding) | ISBN 9798885095396 (paperback) | ISBN 9798885096546 (ebook)
Subjects: LCSH: Wages--Juvenile literature. | Work--Juvenile literature. | Money--Juvenile literature.
Classification: LCC HD4909 .B624 2023 (print) | LCC HD4909 (ebook) | DDC 331.2/1--dc23/eng/20220707
LC record available at https://lccn.loc.gov/2022029717
LC ebook record available at https://lccn.loc.gov/2022029718

For more information, write to Bearport Publishing, 5357 Penn Avenue South, Minneapolis, MN 55419.

Contents

You've Earned It!

You just got paid for babysitting your neighbor's kids. The work was hard, but now you have some money! On the way home, you think about how to spend it. There are so many ways to use money, and there are just as many ways to earn it.

When thinking about how to spend money, pay for needs first. The cell phone you use to get calls about work needs to be paid for. A fun new video game may have to wait.

Off to Work

Whether babysitting or waiting tables, most people make their money at jobs. They are employees who get paid for their time and effort. Employers are the people and businesses who hire employees to work.

At many jobs, employees must be at least 18 years old. However, teens can often work at stores or restaurants. Younger people may make money doing jobs for people they know.

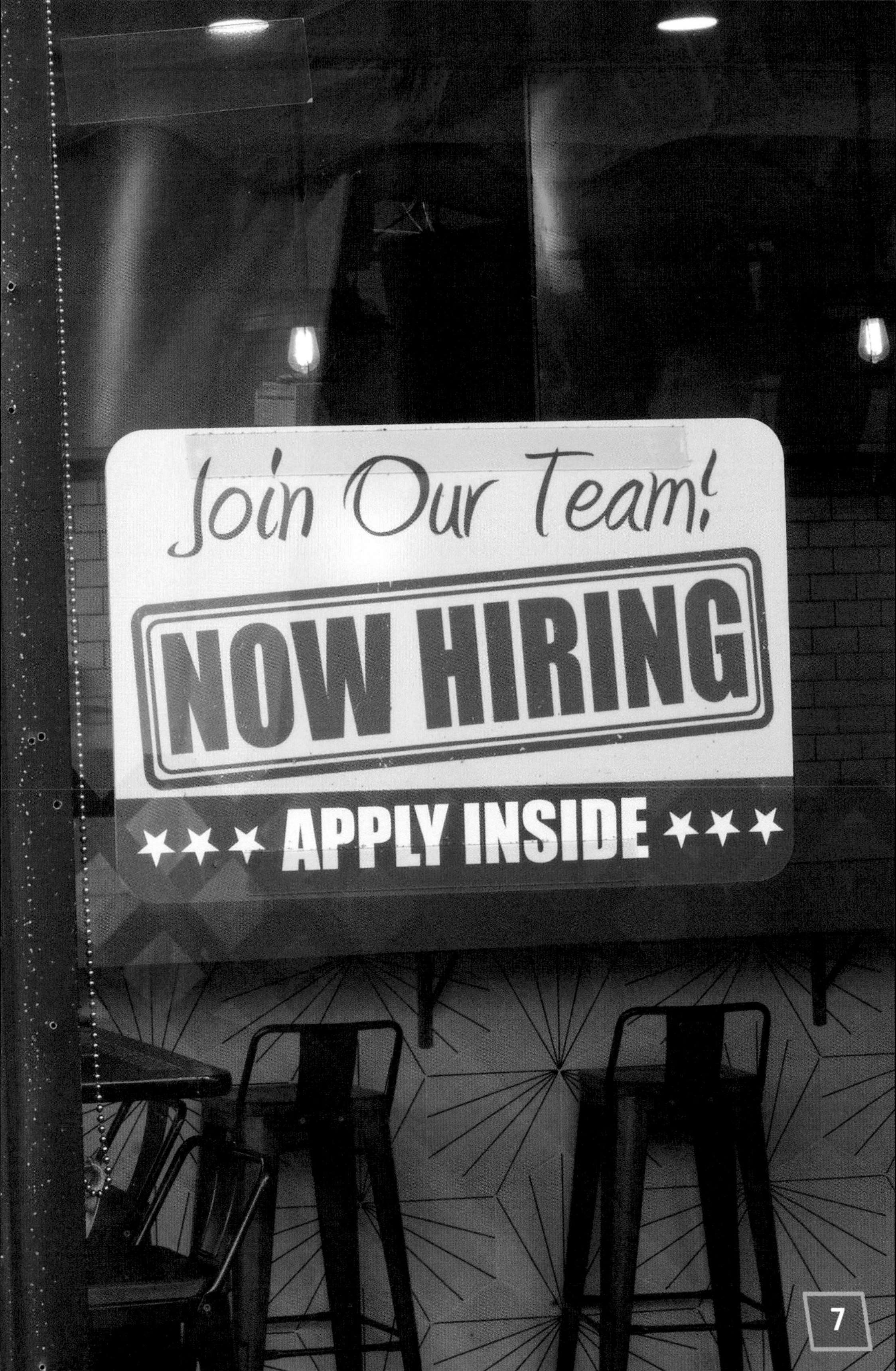
Join Our Team!
NOW HIRING
APPLY INSIDE

Money in Many Ways

How do workers get paid? It depends on the type of job. Some employees make a set amount of money each year. This is called a **salary**. Other workers are paid a **wage**, which is money for each hour they work.

Whether they earn a salary or a wage, most employees get **paychecks** on a regular basis. Each paycheck has a small amount of money taken out for **taxes**. This money goes to the government.

COMPANY INC.
123 Street Name
City Name, CA 90000

Check No: 123456
Client No: 12345

Date: January 10, 2023

Amount: USD 10247.40

Pay against this check
Current Name
Street Name, City

Company Name

Or Order

The Sum of   TEN THOUSAND TWO HUNDRED AND FORTY SEVEN 40/100 U.S. DOLLARS

For: Bank Branch Name

Payable at   Bank Name
Street Name
City Name, CA 90000

Authorized Signature

Take Your Time

How much time an employee works also depends on the job. A person with a full-time job works about 40 hours each week. Others work fewer hours at part-time jobs. This leaves time for other responsibilities, such as going to school. Part-time jobs often pay less than full-time work.

What happens if full-time employees work more than 40 hours? If they earn a wage, they may get overtime pay for the extra hours. This is paid at a higher rate than regular pay.

Some people get temporary jobs called **gigs**. This type of work has flexibility. Gig workers can often choose when and how much they work. Some take enough gigs to work full time. Others may work only a few hours a month.

People who want temporary work can also get seasonal jobs. These jobs last only part of the year. For example, camp counselors usually work only in the summer. A ski resort may hire workers for just the winter.

Photographers, rideshare drivers, and food delivery drivers are often gig workers.

13

Something Extra

Sometimes, workers can earn extra money. One way this happens is when they get tips from customers.

Another kind of extra pay is called a bonus. This comes from employers and can be a reward for doing good work. Bonuses are often given at the end of the year.

Many service workers, such as restaurant servers and hairstylists, get tips. These workers often have low wages. Tips help them earn more money for a job well done.

Tips and bonuses are paid in addition to a wage.

Salespeople sometimes earn pay called commission. This is often in addition to a salary. Commission may be based on how many things a worker sells. The amount can also depend on the price of the items sold.

Real estate agents earn commission. If an agent sells more houses, they can earn more money. They also get more for houses that are more expensive.

Higher Earning

The amount of money a worker earns can also depend on their experience. Employers may pay more to people who have special skills or training. Companies often look for workers who have graduated from high school or college. Some workers, such as electricians and doctors, must have a special **license**.

If employees do their work well, they can sometimes get a **raise**. This is when an employer increases a worker's wage or salary.

Be Your Own Boss

Working for an employer is a good way to earn money. But some people would rather work for themselves. An **entrepreneur** (ahn-truh-pruh-NUR) runs their own business. They sell something or provide a service. Often, business owners start out alone. As their business grows, they will hire employees.

Entrepreneurs usually need money to start a business. Sometimes, they borrow money from a bank. They pay it back after their business starts making money.

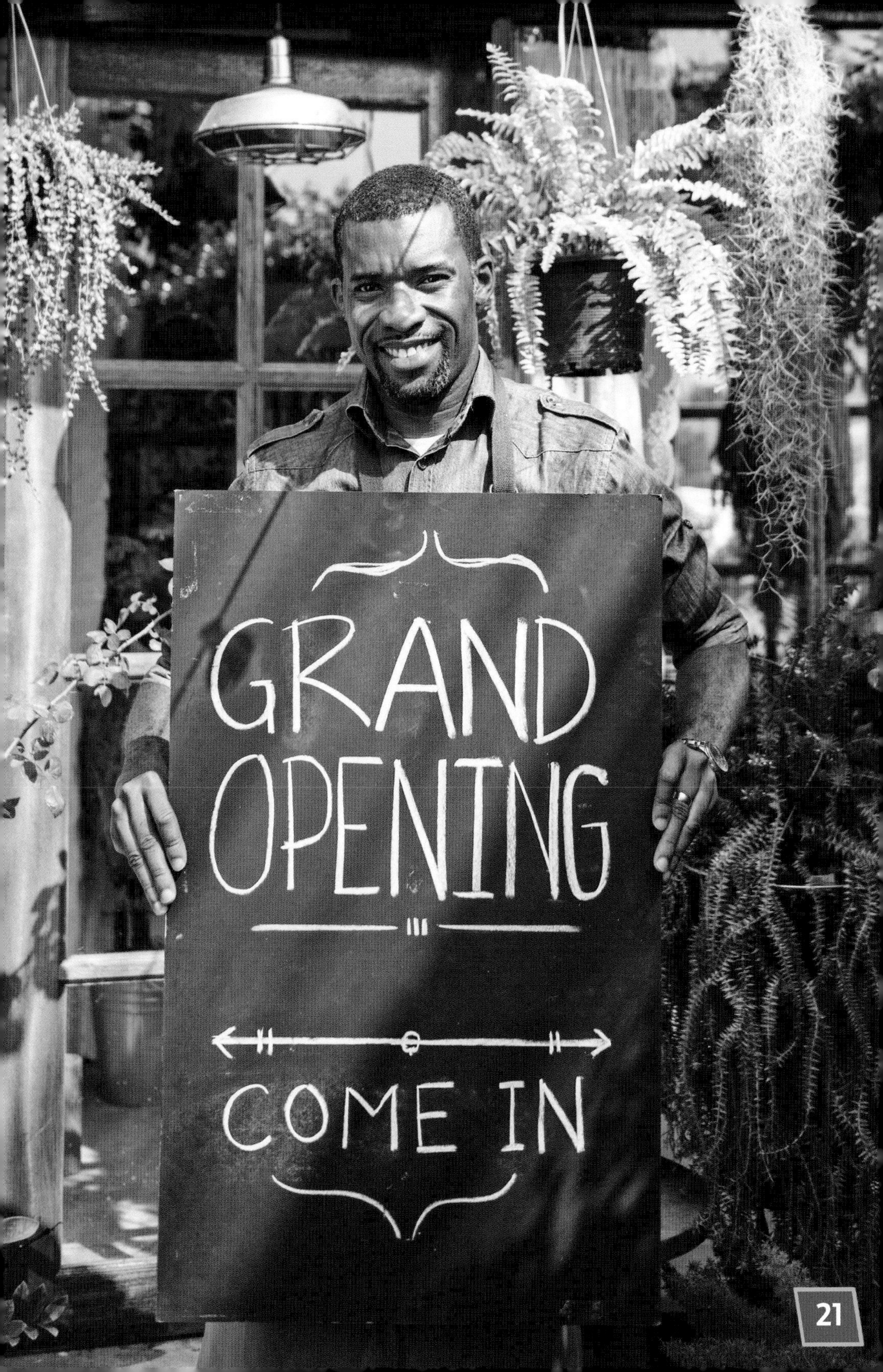
GRAND
OPENING
COME IN

Starting a business means you make money, but you also have to spend it. A business owner has to pay workers and buy supplies. Any money left over is **profit**. This is what the entrepreneur gets to keep. When a business is very successful, the owner gets a lot of money.

Starting a business can be challenging. A lot of new businesses close within five years. Success takes planning, hard work, and a little bit of luck.

Using What You Have

Another way to make money is by renting out things. A person may let others use their home or bike for a price. Like a business owner, the person may spend some of this money to take care of the thing being rented. The rest is profit they get to keep.

How else can you make money with something you own? Try selling it. Many people sell items at yard sales or online.

Money Matters

Making money can be different for everyone. To pay for the costs of daily life, many people need a full-time job. If someone wants extra money to buy something special, they may choose to work extra hours at a gig job. What's the best way for you to make the money you need?

It can take a lot of time and energy to make money. It's not always easy. That's why it's important to spend money wisely.

Ways to Earn

People earn money in different ways depending on the job. Here are some of the ways workers make money.

Wage Workers

Regular Pay

More Money

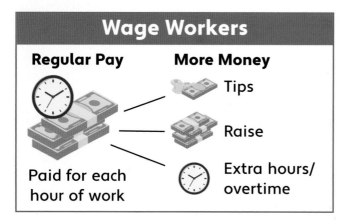

Tips

Raise

Extra hours/overtime

Paid for each hour of work

Salary Workers

Regular Pay

More Money

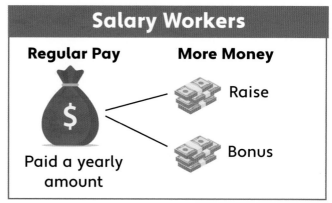

Raise

Bonus

Paid a yearly amount

Commission Workers

Regular Pay

More Money

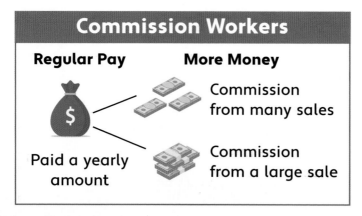

Commission from many sales

Commission from a large sale

Paid a yearly amount

★ SilverTips for REVIEW

Review what you've learned. Use the text to help you.

Define key terms

employee   salary

employer   wage

entrepreneur

Check for understanding

What are two ways people can earn money?

What is the difference between full-time and part-time jobs?

How is an entrepreneur different from an employee?

Think deeper

How are different ways of making money better for different situations?

★ SilverTips on TEST-TAKING

- **Make a study plan.** Ask your teacher what the test is going to cover. Then, set aside time to study a little bit every day.

- **Read all the questions carefully.** Be sure you know what is being asked.

- **Skip any questions** you don't know how to answer right away. Mark them and come back later if you have time.

Glossary

entrepreneur a person who starts their own business

gigs jobs that people can work on a flexible schedule

license a document to show a person can do something

paychecks documents used to pay money to employees

profit the amount of money left after all costs have been paid

raise an increase in the amount someone is paid for their work

salary a set amount of money for a year's worth of work

taxes money people and businesses must pay to the government

wage an amount of money paid for a specific time period, typically hourly

Read More

Hillard, Stephane. *Plan a Babysitting Business (Be Your Own Boss).* New York: PowerKids Press, 2020.

Huddleston, Emma. *Finding a Job (Money Basics).* San Diego, CA: BrightPoint Press, 2020.

Uhl, Xina M. and Daniel E. Harmon. *Getting Your First Job (Managing Your Money and Finances).* New York: Rosen Publishing, 2020.

Learn More Online

1. Go to **www.factsurfer.com** or scan the QR code below.

2. Enter "**Making Money**" into the search box.

3. Click on the cover of this book to see a list of websites.

Index

About the Author

Jennifer Boothroyd's first job was looking after a neighbor's parrot. She has earned money by cleaning, managing, teaching, singing, writing, taking pictures, and caring for children and animals.